THE LAND OF UNLOVING

THE MACMILLAN COMPANY
NEW YORK • CHICAGO
DALLAS • ATLANTA • SAN FRANCISCO
LONDON • MANILA

IN CANADA
BRETT-MACMILLAN LTD.
GALT, ONTARIO

Poems by
Lionel Wiggam

THE LAND OF UNLOVING

New York – The Macmillan Company – 1961

TO MARGARET BURNSIDE

Some of the poems in this volume first appeared in *Landscape with Figures*, Copyright 1936 by Lionel Wiggam.

The three "Fables" are reprinted by permission of the publishers from *Princeton Verse Between Two Wars*, edited by Allen Tate, Copyright 1942 by Princeton University Press.

"The Sky, the Plain, the Pool" is reprinted by permission of the publishers of *Good Housekeeping*.

The poems "Arrowhead," "Music," and "Toyland" originally appeared in *The New Yorker*; "Of Winter" in *Saturday Review*; and "Playground" in *The New York Times*.

First Printing

The Macmillan Company, New York
Brett-Macmillan Ltd., Galt, Ontario

Printed in the United States of America

Library of Congress catalog card number: 61–8267

CONTENTS

I. LANDSCAPE WITH FIGURES

II. THE LAND OF UNLOVING

v

III. THE FLESH

IV. THE POINT OF IT

I. LANDSCAPE WITH FIGURES

SOME WOMEN

Some women walk in wilderness forever.
They live obscurely in a cave of grief.
Their hearts are softly crumbling, as in winter
The blown leaf.

They cannot love, they only may endeavor
To hold with rapture to their hearts the frost;
At length their hearts are pinched until they splinter
And finally are lost.

They fix their lust upon a tangled mountain
And burn the brush and deftly clear the ground.
They are not daunted by the fern or reed,
They work without a sound.

Their passion rises fiercely like a fountain
Till they stare down upon a naked land . . .
Touching a tree near by, or holding a weed
In one tight hand.

IT WAS LIKE THIS

It was like this when I came here last:
Men were intent with fish nets on the bay;
A child gathered shells; a gull fell past
The tallest cliff in a similar way.

Nothing has changed at all, unless the tide
Has advanced ten yards, or receded; I cannot be sure.
But the jellyfish, the same green crabs are beside
The present waves' contour.

I think: it has never changed, and it never will.
The signatures of seaweed are always the same.
Forever there will be this ocean and this hill
As they are now, as they were when first I came:

And in ten or twenty years, if I should return,
The same breakers will burst with the sound like bells,
Revealing the speckled jellyfish, and the ragged fern.
And the child gathering shells.

FABLES

I

Perseus slew the monster, being more
A hero than a poet, unbeguiled
By art and undismayed by gore
And unconfused by how a creature smiled.

But I am I—who humbly wooed the smile
And would not lift my eyes, though well aware.
Your arms encircled me a little while.
I am content: unbind your hair.

II

Implausible in that pale, waning wood,
Offending the twilight, there was Circe; she
At the feathery rim of a fir tree stood:
The shining thing, the shrewd,
Who turned men mindless, gibbering, lewd ...

I seized, I shook her like a bell—
Twisted that softness to me like a stem—
Crying, "Now! Now, work your spell!"

The legend is not true.
Behold: I am no more a swine
Than you, or you.

III

There was a way, by draping gauze
Dipped in holy water over the eyes,
That one could bear whatever the creature was.

Crouched in the thicket, I knew she had come:
The whistling, arrowy birds
Were glued to the branches, suddenly dumb.

So I stood up, confronting her:
Medusa, just as they said.
Hair and eyes, as I had heard they were.

I could love you, were it not for this.
I am not stone, but I have gazed in the eyes
And heard the hair hiss.

ALL MEN ARE PIONEERS

All men are pioneers inside their hearts.
They are forever seeking wilderness.
Behind strong teams they ride in hooded carts,
Avid for life, and masterless.

They would take their women west or north,
They would invade a country terrible with peril,
They would eternally be riding forth
Out of the cities they have found so sterile.

In their hearts they are forever cutting clover,
They are forever drawing water from a well.
In their dreams they are observing, over and over,
The ground they would clear, the forests they would fell.

They are dreaming of lands uncivilized that sprawl
Unfound, or unimagined, or forgot . . .
Knowing they will not leave the town at all,
As like as not.

PHOTOGRAPH OF MY FATHER

Your captured face is innocent of malice:
Serious, thoughtful gaze with eyebrows springing
In soot-black arcs like startled birds upwinging,
The jaws intransigent, the wide mouth guileless.

You seem prepared for any blow at all,
The chin set resolute on its starchy column,
The curls admonished strictly to your skull;
What did you think of things to be so solemn?

The young and forthright face seems any man's.
They say you were kind and brave, admired by many,
They say you loved me, cherished marvelous plans,
And died before you realized any.

PHOTOGRAPH OF MY MOTHER

They took this of you as a bride: you stare,
Straining to look maturer than your teens,
Alertly out, so fervently aware
Of what a marriage means.

A stranger, this, and never known to me,
With lovelocks brushed down richly from a part,
And round cheeks flushed, the color rising free
From the young pump of the heart.

A portentous thing, this posing as a bride;
You wear a brooch, a quiet leaf-shaped thing,
A hat that has no fripperies; while inside
The womanly guise a girl sits quivering.

But you are sure and steadfast, come what may.
Braced on your spine and holding tight your gloves,
You mean to honor, cherish, and obey
Through sickness, health, or even other loves.

And did it prove as awesome as you thought?
And did you learn to harbor every grief
Until it lay as quietly on the heart
As a brooch shaped like a leaf?

SOUTH FIELD

The pasture lies adamant; no blade of grass will yield
To a boy crying in the south field.

There were four perfect creatures, each snug in a shell,
And their mother with a silver bell
Hung in her throat.
They lay in a nest like a strange boat
Under the tall grass.
Today my father let his plow pass
Just above them. I found
Four eggs crushed in furrowed ground,
And the mother on stricken wings
Above the ghastly, ruined things.

I think I shall cry no more in a little while,
And climb over the stile
And go home for my dinner. And next spring the oats
Will hide the earth where the shell was scattered
And four singing throats
Were shattered.

WHEREVER IT WAS

Wherever it was, it was not a city;
It was a shore of granite, perhaps, a place where waves
Assailed the cliffs and gave them angular beauty,
The casual, hard grace that sea gulls have.

There was a forest near it, of hemlock or birch,
And a permanent iron-blue sky was hung above it.
I wandered there, and I slept beneath an arch
Of amber leaves; and I swore I would never leave it.

There was a smell of water and dead brush at night,
A fragrance rank with decay or sweet with moss.
Birds darted among the rocks as swift as thought,
And the serpent that clasped a log was sheer as ice.

It was a place far from here; it was not a city.
It was a shore of granite, and I know the waves
Assailed the cliffs and gave them angular beauty.
These are the only memories I have.

THE SKY, THE PLAIN, THE POOL

We hear their cries at night,
And droppings on the rocks
Confirm their common flight:
The birds fly south in flocks.

The fish explore in schools.
As on a single tether
In ocean deeps and pools
They feed and spawn together.

While on the primitive plain,
By instinct, not by words,
Through dust and drought and rain,
The wild beasts go in herds.

The sky, the plain, the pool:
Love, love, where shall we find
The flock or herd or school
Of our own kind?

FOR HIS FATHER

Sleep in the still, green grass, and when the rain
Pursues the impartial pattern of your breast,
Think of a helpless groping boy again,
The fire beneath his lids, the manifest
Desire upon his body, and the pain
That slides more sure than blood beneath his chest.

Never having been alone, he finds
The skyward-sloping hills too steep to measure
The angle of his heart, the similar winds
Too swift and counterfeit to cool the treasure
Burning behind his brow, and learns how blest
The faded bone is, and the uncoiled vein,
Being secure, and being happiest.

THIS MOUNTAIN IS MY PROPERTY

This mountain is my property alone:
A hard expanse of cocklebur and pines,
A lace of grass subsiding into stone,
And overhead a purple fret of vines.

These are my woods, and this my personal scene:
Where fallen underfoot the balsam boughs
And partridge feathers pattern each ravine,
And where the hornet plots his paper house.

For no man knows this place so well as I;
Not one has seen this roof of branches torn
By sun, or watched the overhanging sky
Scraped by a wing as sharply as a thorn.

This place is mine, where evening breeds alarm:
A thin disquiet sharpened with despair,
Where dusk approaches like a locust swarm
Spreading its copper rumor down the air.

From here I came, and here I must return,
A rightful habitant to claim his own.
As any sharp-eyed creature's in the fern,
This mountain is my property alone.

II. THE LAND OF UNLOVING

TOYLAND

The land where children live is full of rage,
Felons and murderers there grow strong and tall,
And all your pitiful love cannot assuage
These Lears in miniature, Macbeths in small.

You have conceived, perhaps, a rosy place,
Finding the doll tucked sweetly in its wagon,
Or Gothic world of gallantry and grace,
With nothing eviler in it than a dragon.

Your nursery closet bulges with its dead—
A score of slaughtered persons with no mourner.
As like as not, you'd find your own poor head
Tossed in a corner.

THIS SCENE IS FROZEN

This scene is frozen in a sharp hiatus;
Nothing again will ever happen here.
Always this balanced meadow will await us,
The sun unsinking, the horizon sheer.

Always the bat will wheel above the river,
The rabbit be pursued, the fox pursue.
Always the tapered willow leaves will quiver,
The sweet fern touch the fence unchanged and true.

By time forgot the cows will crop the grasses,
The sheep begin and then forget to bleat,
The branches bend for wind that never passes,
The crabbed buzzard pause on crooked feet.

Forever I shall stand here stonyhearted,
Watching you climb the high hill opposite,
My hand forever reaching, my lips parted
To say the word, but never saying it.

STRUGGLE

Being less of man than elf,
A boy must overcome himself.
Let him flee, or let him fight,
Let him struggle through the night.

His cheek will grow a golden beard,
Symbol of the thing he feared.
His voice will find a lower note
And stifle boyhood in his throat.

Oh, he must overcome the joy,
The laughter of that other boy,
And beat him down, and see surprise
Rise in his stricken, loving eyes.

Until, articulate and sad,
He turns away the other lad;
And seeks a dark forgotten place
To hide his weeping face.

OF WINTER

To M. K. B.

That day I walked through a city locked in ice.
Rain before dawn had frozen where it fell,
Clasping each object in a glittering vise,
Sealing all things inside a crystal shell.

Here was a miracle marvelous as spring:
To find a city's bones turned blond and brittle.
Fireplugs and lampposts, every mundane thing,
Crusted and sheathed and luminous a little.

It seemed they must break, each iridescent structure,
The paperweight city must come crashing down.
One tremor of light, one shiver of sound would puncture
The whole fantasia, raze the improbable town. . . .

Then I recalled another ice-locked country,
A landscape frigid but in no wise frail,
The place where a heart depended, fixed and wintry,
Frozenly shrouded, locked in a glassier mail.

The city, I thought, will presently thaw, not splinter,
Unlike the heart to any summer lost,
Unlike the heart that cherishes its winter
And hugs its frost.

STEPHEN'S SON

This child is ponderous with terrible wisdom:
At ten all knowledge is behind his stare,
Austere, remotely grave, he lives in secret.
We would approach the boy, but scarcely dare.

On misty afternoons we hear him shouting,
Playing his lonely games across the field.
But silently he comes home for his supper:
We smile and speak, but he will never yield.

Something within his voice, his eyes, reproves us.
He stares aloof on unfamiliar scene.
Our invitations he refuses firmly.
In some mysterious world he moves serene.

His father died before his mother bore him:
"Perhaps," she sighs, "if Stephen were not dead . . ."
And then she weeps, observing the cold gestures,
The alien dignity, the curious proud head.

ARROWHEAD

The history books are true; today I found
This piece of flint among the maidenhair.
The heart it penetrated with no sound
Released this symbol when it crumbled there.

Barbaric hands with murderous intent
Chiseled this indentation like a star;
Piercing the evening-colored air it went,
Whistling and savagely triangular.

With deft precision was the hard point made,
And terror struck the heart that heard it come.
And he was terrible and unafraid
Who drew the bowstring taut beneath his thumb:

Gentle and piteous the doe or hare
That sprang bewildered with the fang of death
Spraying its tender blood on twilight air,
Halting its innocent breath.

PLAYGROUND

The sagebrush in these parts is loud with rattlers,
The hills bear castles Merlin has in thrall,
And over there some Sioux besiege some settlers,
And over there some powerful mobsters sprawl.

The girls with atom guns across their laps
Are grim Cassandras chanting right and wrong,
The brooding boys in decorated chaps
Are Hamlets in the guise of Hopalong.

Here is the stuff of Tolstoi and Racine
Juiced up to fit the times, the plots of Poe
And Sophocles heightened as by benzedrine:
Dick Tracy helps Aeneas through the snow.

Venus and Xanadu, Sherwood Forest, Oz,
The world is razed and rendered as it could be;
Adults who pause here see it as it was
And as it should be:

Where Sugar Ray and Lancelot pull their punch,
Where skewered steeds arise to foal again,
Where strangled heroes yammer for their lunch,
And bombed-out cities spring up whole again.

SNOW IS THE KINDEST

Snow is the kindest of all natural things,
Affording the rabbit camouflage, the trout a roof,
Dimming the grouse, obscuring the pheasant's wings,
Paling the antler, hiding the printed hoof.

There is no view it cannot render charming;
Ruins and dumps become felicities,
Gravestones and gravel pits become disarming,
And the stark limbs of trees.

No bed is so voluptuous to lie in.
Have you no home? Are you fed up and spent?
Few arms there are so soft as these to die in.
Ponder the virtues of this element.

No whisper is so sweet as snow falling.
No touch of a tender woman tenderer.
It is a lover; have you not heard it calling?
You could do worse than answer, wanderer.

CHASE

We never dreamed the happy chase
Would end in that disturbing place:
Green, quiet cave with pines that were
A roof above its singular guest—
He with a faun's alarming face,
He with a boy's thin, angular breast
Subsiding into fur.

We thought to find a worried fox
Observing us with blazing eyes
Behind an ambuscade of rocks;
Until we saw the hounds withdraw,
Disclosing that improbable head
And hoofs all torn: until we saw
A bleeding pixy face, instead.
And then, like us, the hounds that were
Suddenly grown quieter.

GROWTH

Being a child was being joyously wanton,
Happy to have no conscience, giddy with greed;
A season's riches were all the presents gotten,
The pennies pilfered, the vile, unpunished deed.

The kitten stoned had little to match the charm of.
Pleasure was drowning at length the litter's runt.
Fun was a frailer child to twist the arm of,
Or the lady who lived in the house with elms in front.

Hers was a face all blazing and disarrayed,
With mild wild eyes that burned from an upstairs window;
We stood at the curb and laughed at the fool she played
With her addled tears and mouthings that made us tingle.

But once adult, of course, we have grown more human.
We steal with remorse, and slay with decent warning.
And the face at the window is merely that of a woman
We turn at the curb to wave to every morning.

UNICORN

To H. A.

Love is no cupid on a valentine,
Replete with misty lace and scalloped edges:
Love is a beast, relentless and malign,
That paces stony shelves and thorny ledges.
Love stalks the mountain, silent and aloof;
Love is the legendary unicorn,
An ancient beast that has a heart-shaped hoof
And on his brow a single spiral horn.
And you will see him not, though he is there,
Nor will you hear his soft, impatient tread;
And when you venture near, all unaware,
Love will be crouching quietly overhead:
And soon that cold, malicious beast will spring
And in your heart his pointed horn will sting.

III. THE FLESH

FIRST LOVE

The girl who has taken her first lover
Assumes at once a dignity and pride.
The haughty queen is no more proud than she,
The tyrant-empress no more dignified.

Her heart is a strange wing, stirring and subsiding;
She turns to mountains, then she wanders south.
Nothing remotely pacifies her anguish,
Save her lover's mouth.

Her friends will question her, but she is distant:
Careful to keep her fear unmanifest.
She coolly smiles, her piteous avid heart
A wild and fluttering thing inside her breast.

Only her lover silences that panic.
Only his touch, his smile, subdue the grief.
Running to meet him, she is a child who whispers:
"Look! I have brought you a curious heart-shaped leaf."

LOT

Before me lies a vast plain
Flanked by hills and worried waters.
Intrepidly I face the rain,
I, and my weeping daughters,
Daring not to breathe her name,
She who must admire
The excellence of flowering flame,
The leering face of fire.

The darkness sighs and slides apart,
And lets us penetrate its heart.
Even the grass, the sable grass,
Cleaves itself to let us pass.

Almost, I think, my heart will burst,
My throat be torn with grief;
I see her as she stood at first,
Her mouth a trembling leaf—
And then the brow superb in salt,
The ankle sloping into pillar,
The surging pulse's secret halt,
The quivering mouth becoming stiller.

THE CLOWN

To W. E.

How I would free you, as all the ones before you,
From these old rites whereby I drag us down.
Love, listen. I implore you,
Know what we kneel to is a clown.

Ribald with popping eyes and purple skull
And ochre mouth that sniggers and grimaces,
He cuts his capers for any candle at all,
And makes his faces.

Here in my heart is his altar built,
Here as a boy I made my first devotions,
To see him put on his coat of crazy quilt
And launch his outlandish motions.

And here I brought my earliest love, as you,
To murmur with me the prayers that make him jig,
And flap his arms till the crazy quilt's askew,
And squeal like a pig.

Know what we worship as a clown, I beg you,
Know in my heart the creature actually there,
Who for your love will shimmy as with ague,
Or comically stare.

There is no child, as I have said,
Weeping and scared and helpless to utter a sound,
There is a noisy caperer, instead,
A clown.

SHE PREFERS NOT TO PONDER

She prefers not to ponder what may come to pass.
Her small concentric brain cell never musters
A barricade of thought for Time: the glass
She gazes into proves her hair is lustrous.

She does not brood how she must yield to years,
Or how a wrinkle works alarming evil.
Her smile is candid, with no pause for tears,
Her stare is lovely, confident and level.

Her day is given to the problem how
She can remake a last-year's dress most smartly.
She reckons not with anything but Now,
Turning a delicate ear to praise alertly.

I would congratulate her saying, "Youth
Is a matter of necklaces and hairdress wholly;
Age is an old-wives' tale, a legend: Truth
Is a clever theory, but disproven, really."

CURIOUS AND PROFOUND

Curious and profound
Her slender fingers bend,
Moving without sound
To beckon or extend.

The radiant crafty brain
Watchfully directs them;
They err, and piercing pain
Relentlessly corrects them.

Until they learn to press
Disarmingly a wrist
With cunning tenderness,
And then, to seize, to twist,

To break with savage force!
Till ruined and dismissed
To drop with no remorse,
Unpitied and unkissed.

THIRD-FLOOR REAR

The third-floor rear, fed up last night, cut loose
With a fifth of gin and a breastful of abuse
And a safety razor blade, and they say her bath
Is a technicolor photo of all her wrath.

We knew her as a fairish, oldish creature,
Doubtful of manner, nondescript of feature,
Pushing aside her hair like dried-out grass
And lingering on the landings to let us pass.

No one was ever so courteous or docile,
Looking askance at us and shifting her parcel,
Clearing her throat, too timid to say a greeting,
Or, if she did, it was more like a small sheep bleating.

So we couldn't have been so shocked if the ceiling fell,
And nobody called the cops when she started to yell;
Her hoots and swear words made the whole house tremble,
And everyone, even the gentlemen basement-front, got a sample.

Oh, how she hated us behind those little gold earrings,
And that ratty old fur piece and those low throat clearings,
And this morning her bathroom's a dazzling dream of colors
Spewed out from those wrists as delicate as crullers.

Blood on the floor and walls, says the landlord, the ceiling, even,
Where she flung up her bursting wrists and howled at heaven,
And we huddle like churchgoers in the hallways, hushed and awed
At someone who scared herself even more than God.

SONNET

To M. B. W.

Love was our object, not its mystery
Or what might lie past tenderness and touch.
Recalling, now, the witless history,
I can't despise our simple ardor much.
Love is a ways and means for larger people,
Chopin snatched music from it, Sand a book;
We sought no further reach of good or evil
Beyond the fingers' clutch, the eyes' look.

The thought of what's to come was dim as weather
Or smears across a lunar landscape strewn.
Alone we were, then suddenly together,
Catching each other close within the ruin.
We clasped and kissed and asked no kind of wherefore.
We said, It's dark, I'm lost. I love you therefore.

THE SKILLFUL HUNTSMAN

Today I carved this arrow:
  A simple thing to lift.
So light it is, and narrow,
  So arrogantly swift.

While languid in the quiver
  It seems a harmless thing,
Inadequate to sever
  A lean flank or a wing;

But quickly and discreetly
  And deftly it can kill!
For no bird flies so fleetly . . .
  Wait yonder on the hill,

And I shall bring you plunder:
  Perhaps a soft-eyed doe,
The small heart torn asunder,
  Immaculately so!

THE UNLOVED WOMAN

The unloved woman in love, like a refugee, takes
Whatever route is at hand, whether south or west.
Familiars are suddenly foreigners; she forsakes
Her dearest environs, adrift and dispossessed.

The wild, blown leaf in her breast is her only friend,
And any wind lifting the buffeted thing, she follows.
You will encounter her shuddering toward the wind,
Or, when it dies, like a spent bird in the shallows.

There is no path for her anywhere but the wind's;
It whispers outside her door, or pleads and hisses;
She must abandon you, then, with all her friends,
Unable to stop her ears up like Ulysses.

When the weather is calm, you can counsel her a little;
She answers lucidly, assents and nods,
But only a draft down the stair or a shaken petal
Can plunge her forth with a purpose fierce as God's,

To be the wind's own total creature, flung
She knows not where but longs to discover, at most,
The mist of his palm on a rail, or a song he's sung
Diminishing off down a corridor like a ghost.

STRANGER

I know a boy whose eyes are large with secrets;
Their olive innocence is softly veiled.
We see him from our window, climbing hill crests,
Alone and silent; somehow, we have failed.
For he is unyielding, cold, and we are powerless.
He is forever proof to all our guiles.
We cannot bribe his love with sweets or marbles,
Nor tease him from his reticence with smiles.

But sometimes I would tell him: Keep your council.
We should respect your secrets, having none.
Yours is the day's bright gold, and ours its tinsel.
Yours is the mystery which for us is done.

Keep your boy's dignity, be cold and strange.
And break our stupid hearts. But do not change.

DERELICT

He is forsaken, now: he grieves.
He restlessly strolls the impassive field in wonder.
He broods by the fountain; he lies under
The tree that lifts an artifice of leaves.

He cannot forget, try as he will.
He would become the beast, wild and debased,
The serpent, the stag; but uneffaced
Her mouth still taunts him past the farthest hill.

No shape he assumes can dispossess
The specter: whether he be the hound and harry,
Or the frightened fox, pursued and wary—
He can elude her never, nonetheless.

He looks to the stars, and meets her stare.
He listens, and thinks: the flutter of leaves falling.
It is her voice, and she is calling.
He rages, rises, flees; she is anywhere.

IV. THE POINT OF IT

MUSIC

Music becomes intolerable, indeed,
After the violins are stopped,
After
The keys are quiet and the reeds
Are put aside. Before the laughter
And flutter of applause, there is a space:
Before the sudden rush of clattering palms:
A briefest hush impossible to trace.

The symphony is done. The maestro bows.
Yet in that pause
Before he turns, you hear it.
Not an echo, or a note
Ineffable and remote:
But simply a soundlessness before the people rise
And disenchant themselves with their own cries.

ROOTED IN ROCK

From stone the milkweed builds its frosty parts,
And why it struggles so is not made clear;
The hawthorn branches lift from colored quartz,
And vines persist though flint would interfere.
How aromatic mint devised itself
In sullen crevices, it does not say;
And thus the wild grape on a granite shelf
Trails over it the tendrils' disarray.
And these are strange, but this is stranger still:
Why any man will bring his woman here,
Build graceless shelter on an open hill
For storms to break upon, and persevere.
Rooted in rock, perhaps, he sees the rose,
And builds thereby, though why he scarcely knows.

MATHEMATICS

Child, behold the lovely pattern
Mars and Venus draw with Saturn.
Pause upon a hill and see
Celestial geometry.

Bend and carefully observe
The petal's precise fabric curve.
This is mathematics true
Beyond the kind that men construe.

Any vine you gaze upon
Plots a perfect pentagon.
Every ray the sun expels
Fashions faultless parallels.

Where the comet wanes and comes
Are essential axioms.
Gaze upon the sky, and ponder—
Primal algebra is yonder.

SONNETS

I

We are forsworn: the high and circling wing,
The pendulous grape precisely drawn to scale,
The imperious antler lifted to the spring,
The silver weed, the creeping, thrice-coiled snail.
We are forsworn: the timorous opening rose,
The diffident fawn descending to the stream,
The delicate shells that in the sea unclose,
The languorous leaves that drift and wetly gleam.
Nothing rebels: the ascendant rose must halt,
The wing and weed be indiscriminately rust,
The grape turn bitter, and the shell turn salt,
The heart that loves them be accounted dust:
The heart that loves them be accounted less
Than air, than space, than utter nothingness.

II

As any paradox of thorn and petal,
As any wistful tenant of the grass,
As even the proud beast, the small nettle:
This treason even love cannot surpass.
The serpent and the stag will yield together,
The ample bough, the snugly curling root,
The fallen blossom and the fallen feather,
And you, as well, will crumble underfoot.
And in that hour not even love can stay you,
No passionate prayer or promise can revise
The scheme that planned you only to betray you,
Leveling you to a landscape's fall and rise:
No less or more availing, in that hour,
Than any casual fern or quiet flower.

48

IN A GARDEN

Here, in secret, darts the spider
With an image-freezing face,
Looping on the thistle's fiber
Fatal strands of lace.
Spun incredibly of peril
Underneath the nettle stem,
Lifting dew like globes of beryl,
Swings his stratagem.

Here is beauty of precision:
Glinting water set on gauze.
Here the monster, in derision,
With a head of claws
Guards his lovely architecture:
Air-thin rope upholding dew;
From his thoughtful bowel the structure
Curve-on-spiral grew....

Innocent wing and guileless eyes,
Small, infatuate things, beware ...
Death in luminous disguise
Is hovering there.

THE CRAG

Climb to the crag that only eagles know,
And let your eye observe a vortex down,
Down to the ocean's image miles below,
The forest done in miniature, the town.

Climb to the bluff, and see your friend become
A speck upon the underlying shale,
A grain of dust to crumble with your thumb,
An ant to crush beneath your fingernail.

And those who towered above you now are mites.
This is a place forevermore to dim
All littler altitudes and lesser heights:
Now you are God, or very close to Him.

AS FALLING FROST

A man is fortunate indeed
Who grieves at night for something lost.
Who cannot sleep, nor rise and read . . .
When delicately as falling frost
Or tenderly as murmured words,
There comes the harmony of birds.

A strange, a soft, compelling sound . . .
A gift for any man who grieves.
The feathery song will lock him round,
As lightly falling as the leaves.
Until in spite of tears he lies
While one inquires and one replies.

Not even rain can come so still
As this contagion in the night
Of birds who call from hill to hill.
A man who hears must heed in spite
Of ruthless sorrow or despair
Or love's most cold and cunning snare.

Until at last the birds are gone.
Nor is he positive he heard
The net of mystic sound; the dawn
Has left the fragile echo blurred.
He lies amazed; almost it seems
They were not birds at all, but dreams.

A MAN WITHOUT WILDERNESS

To A. L. H.

A man without wilderness to challenge him
Is a strong blade rusting in a corner.
His thighs are curved to fit a saddle,
His hands are shaped to hold a harness rein.
A man without miles of brush to clear
Is a field that gives no grain.

A man without brambles to tear his fingers
Before he can sow a stretch of earth with seed
Is a plow that crumbles in a farmyard.
His mind must think in terms of harvest yield,
His ear listen to axles turning,
His eyes compute the stacked sheaves to a field.

There must be peril imminent about him;
He must hear water, restless and rebellious;
He must see thorns beyond his window sill,
Sharp to bring his blood.
A man without mountains on his horizon
Is an ax that cleaves no wood.

THE HIGH HILL

Time stopped breathless just below the summit.
Curving apples halted on the air.
The sky retained the cold kiss of a comet.
A weasel's darting glance became a stare.

Tight green buds delayed their bloom.
Bees on a lily's lip were stricken clinging.
The wind with mild surprise did not resume
Its worried singing.

All my length was frozen briefly;
My heart hung strangely heavy like a plummet.
Everything delayed, my still heart chiefly.
And then I moved again, and topped the summit.

IN PRAISE OF DELAY

To J. P. K.

Being a child was knowing the present pain
Would never end.
Time taught you you would breathe again.
Time proved, in time, your dearest friend.

Obscuring issues as it did, the breaking
Of vows of love or treaties in the making.

Remember the letter you could not bear to read?
Remember the various wars when they were newest?
The longer you lived, of all good things, indeed,
Time was the truest.

It is better, always, perhaps, to wait—
To let time have its way—
Especially we who are inclined to act too late
Or speak when there is nothing left to say.

BYSTANDER

What trees have risen slim and green,
What comet stopped in shattered flight,
What things my eyes have never seen,
I am not troubled by tonight.

I stroll indifferent in rain
Or unconcerned I lie in grass,
Watching the moon appear and wane,
Feeling the seasons come and pass.

In other towns are men who brood
On creatures nondescript and dead:
If there is chaos in my mood,
It is for living things instead.

CONCLUSIONS

I

He climbs a hill and turns his face
Impudently into space.
He builds a tower that he may climb
Higher still, and measure time.
He fixes Vega, contemplates
Orion, shrewdly calculates
The moon; assembling what he saw
He arrogantly makes a law.
But never can he build a tower
From which to see what passions are.
He cannot fix and name the course
His own heart takes, though he explores
The whole amazing length of heaven.
He is forever baffled; even
Though he knows how worlds evolve,
Himself he cannot solve.

II

No more than any sea shell cast
By waves upon a beach,
Shining softly in the sun,
Beyond the water's reach,
Is he; as unimportantly
Against the earth he glistens;
He makes a similar noise to
The idle ear that listens.
For hold your ear against his chest:
What does a heartbeat tell?
Nothing less or nothing more
Than any cockleshell.

III

The fable: flesh will crumble with
The hills—he fancies this a myth
He cannot dare; that blood will surge
Out from his mortal veins and merge
With oceantides, he will not credit.
Terror too great to contemplate
Is that wild dream when blood will run
Among the roots, or flesh be spun
An intimate counterpart of grass.
Too darkly great to meditate
Is such a legend; when the glass
Records with sand how time subsides,
He will be listening to the tides,
He will be walking where the snow
Descends significantly slow.